# Built On Faith

## My First Years As A Realtor

### Blake Osman

Krypton Publishing

Published by Krypton Publishing

kryptonpublishing@gmail.com

ISBN: 979-8-9986948-5-1 (eBook)

ISBN: 979-8-9986948-4-4 (Paperback)

ISBN: 979-8-9986948-6-8 (Hardcover)

First Printed Edition 2026

Please take the time to leave a honest review of this book. You can do so by searching it on Amazon.com, go towards the bottom of the page and you should see "write a review." Thank you for your support!

**Author Email**

BlakeOsman50@gmail.com

**Author Website**

BlakeOsmanBooks.com

BlakeOsman.com

For all who walked beside me on this journey of faith;
your prayers, presence, and your words of hope
became stepping stones on the path back to God.


To Laci,
whose faith never wavered,
quiet strength carried us forward,
and whose love held me steady through every storm.


To Braden, Mikyla, and Logan,
your lives spoke louder than sermons,
gently guiding me home to the Father
with every act of love and grace.


To every soul who urged me to trust,
believe, and take the next step in faith,
this book is a testament to your light.
With all my love, and by God's grace, thank you.

# Contents


1.  "The Grind Before the Calling" — 1

2.  "When the Body Breaks" — 5

3.  "Another Door Opens" — 9

4.  "Mind Set" — 14

5.  "Faith in the Follow-Up" — 19

6.  "Plant the Seeds" — 25

7.  "First Fruit of the Calling" — 31

8.  "Baptism by Fire" — 35

9.  "Faithful in the Slow Season" — 38

10.  "Obedience Leads to Overflow" — 42

11.  "Building for More Than Me" — 45

12.  "What the First Year Actually Looks Like" — 48

13.  "Your First 100 Days: Strategy, Systems, and Sanity" — 51

14.  "The Real Costs of Being a Realtor" — 54

15.  "Powerful Prospecting Activities" — 57

16.  "Building Relationships, Not Just a Database" — 62

17.  "The Power of Multiple Streams of Income" — 66

18. "Built on Faith – Daily Devotionals"  69

19. "Faith in the Storm: Thriving in a Difficult Market"  72

20. "Standing Firm When It's Hard"  75

21. "From Broken to Built"  78

22. Final Thought To You, the Reader… The One Who's Still Building  84

Acknowledgements  86

About the author  87

Also by  89

# Chapter One

# "The Grind Before the Calling"

*How long will you ignore God's whisper?*

The year was 1995, I was young, ambitious, and ready to conquer the world. I had just started a job as a delivery driver for one of the world's largest shipping companies, but in my heart, I knew I was meant for more.

What I didn't know yet was God had dreams for me too; bigger, better, and far beyond what I was trying to force in my own strength. Looking back, I can see how He was already planting seeds; in my ambition, in my curiosity, and even in my frustration when things didn't go as planned.

That delivery route became more than a job. It became the first step on a long path where God would strip away my pride, rebuild my purpose, and eventually lead me into real estate.

Over the years, like many people who start a job full of fire and vision, I began to feel the slow, grinding weight of routine. The ambition that once lit me up started to dim. I was no longer waking up with a purpose. Instead, I was clocking in and praying the day would go quickly.

Burnout crept in silently as I questioned everything. Was this really all there was? The same routes, the same stress, the same dreams sitting on the shelf.

Long hours and long years blurred together in a job that paid the bills, but quietly emptied my soul. On paper, I was doing what I was supposed to do… providing, showing up, keeping the lights on. But deep inside, I was worn thin by the weight of quiet dissatisfaction.

I was working 12 to 14-hour days, and somewhere in that grind, life kept racing ahead without me. My kids were growing faster than I could keep up. Milestones came and went, memories were being made, and I felt nothing more than a tired shadow passing through it all. With that, I started to feel the ache of what I was missing. I wasn't just drained, I was grieving the life I thought I was supposed to be living.

During all of this, I stumbled upon *Think and Grow Rich by Napoleon Hill*, and it lit a fire within me. The idea that I could <u>think</u> my way into a better future had me dreaming wide awake. I believed with enough hustle, I could achieve anything.

And it hurt.

I remember sitting in my truck after a long shift, hands on the steering wheel, too exhausted to even start the engine, and whispering a quiet prayer: *"God… is this really it? Is this all there is?"*

I believe God hears even our most tired prayers, and sometimes, He uses dissatisfaction not to punish us, but to prepare us. I didn't know it yet, but He was stirring something new in me. Something better. A calling I hadn't considered on my own. A future I hadn't imagined. While I couldn't see it clearly, something in my spirit whispered: *There's more.*

Now let's get this straight…I didn't hear an audible voice. There was no lightning bolt or dramatic sign in the sky. Simply one day, while scrolling aimlessly through my phone on a lunch break, something caught my eye. A simple ad for a local real estate class. Just a link and a line:

*"Tired of working for someone else? Start your own journey in Real Estate."*

It was nothing special, but it stirred something in me, just a slight tug, a tiny flicker of interest. I almost scrolled past it, but instead I whispered, *"Lord… could this be something?"*

That night, I couldn't seem to shake it. Real estate kept showing up on TV, in random conversations, and even in articles I wasn't looking for. It was like the universe was echoing something that my spirit already knew… but my mind wasn't quite ready to hear.

Then I picked up a book I had heard about for years but never read: *The Purpose Driven Life by Rick Warren.*

That book wrecked me. I don't mean a soft nudge or a friendly reminder, I mean full-on conviction. It was like Rick Warren reached through the pages, grabbed me by the collar and said, "You were made for more."

Something deep inside cracked open. I knew, without a doubt, God was calling me to more. I knew He had placed something in me that had nothing to do with a paycheck and everything to do with a purpose.

This was the defining moment. The one I thought I'd been waiting for. But here's the truth no one likes to say out loud, I didn't change a thing. I kept waking up, clocking in, and pushing through another day of doing what I knew wasn't aligned with who I was becoming.

That day of change would come, but not yet, not for another few years.

Obedience comes at a cost, and at that point in my life, I still feared the cost more than I trusted the Caller.

It would be years of the same old thing. Yes, I moved around within the company, chasing titles, trying to climb a ladder I wasn't even sure I wanted to be on. Promotions came, responsibilities shifted, but deep down, it all felt… empty. Like I was wearing shoes that didn't fit, walking a path that wasn't mine.

Looking back now, I can clearly see the signs. God was speaking the whole time: *"Have faith. Trust Me and step out."* But I didn't. That gentle prompting would rise in my spirit, again and again, but I kept stuffing it down.

*"It's not time yet, God. Let me get my finances right first. I need more experience."*

The truth? I was afraid. I was stubborn. I told God I trusted Him, but my actions said otherwise. I acted as if I had the complete blueprint, as if I knew best. I kept choosing safety over surrender. Yet, despite my resistance, God remained patient. He never stopped calling. He just kept whispering: *"When you're ready, I'm still here."*

# Chapter Two

# "When the Body Breaks"

On a frozen interstate in the dead of winter 2013, everything changed. A man, clearly in a bigger hurry than I was, tried to pass me on an ice-covered road. In a split second, his vehicle lost control and slammed into mine. The force of the impact whipped my body one way and my neck the other. I knew something was wrong immediately.

The result? Herniated discs in my cervical spine.

The outcome? Neck fusion surgery, months of recovery, and pain that lingered long after the scars had healed. For a brief moment, just a flicker of clarity in the middle of all that pain, I told myself: *"This is it. This is the sign. It's time to step out on faith. Go chase what God put in your heart."* I didn't listen. After months of rehab and reflection, I walked right back into the same job, the same routine, the same safety net I'd been tangled in for years. Another seven years passed, seven years of aching through workdays, not just in my body, but in my spirit.

Through it all, God kept speaking.

*"It's time. Have faith. I've called you to more."* But I didn't listen. Not because I didn't believe He was speaking, but because I didn't believe I was ready.

2020 changed everything.

The world was spinning in chaos, COVID, lockdowns, fear, and isolation. Everyone was walking around raw and on edge, just trying to survive the next headline. Navigating that alone was hard enough. But while the world unraveled outside, something inside me was quietly breaking too.

I'd love to say my next moment of reckoning came during something heroic…skydiving, surfing, climbing a mountain, but the truth was far less dramatic. I was doing what I'd always done. Working. Hustling. Carrying the weight… literally.

I was on my route, performing my regular courier duties, when I went to lift an abnormally large box. The moment I pulled it off the ground, I felt something shift, something sharp, immediate, and profound. I told myself it was nothing – just a pulled muscle, maybe a strain. Annoying, sure, but minor. I'd worked through worse. Ice it, rest a bit, power through. That was the plan. Turns out, I had no idea what I was dealing with.

After months of therapy, tests, and stubborn denial, the truth finally came to the surface: the discs in my neck, from C4 to C7, had ruptured. This time, it wasn't just my neck; we were going to add my lower back into the mix.

The only solution was another spinal fusion surgery. This time, I broke. Not just physically broken… mentally, emotionally, and
spiritually broken.

This wasn't just another injury; it was the straw that broke the camel's back. I had come to the end of myself. All the signs God had been placing before me over the years… the whisper to step out in faith… the calling I had buried again and again… Suddenly, it all rose to the surface.

This pain wasn't punishment. It was permission. Permission to finally let go, and step into what God had been preparing me for all along.

After my surgery in March of 2021, the following year became one long road of recovery… physically, mentally, and spiritually. Healing wasn't linear. It was rough, and I sank into a deep depression. My body would never be the same again, and I knew it. I didn't feel like the man I used to be, and some days, I wasn't sure who I was becoming. It was a bitter pill to swallow. But in that dark and painful season, God gave me a secret weapon…my wife.

If it weren't for her, I don't know if I would've made it out with my mind intact. She was my anchor. My encourager and my daily reminder to keep going. She didn't let me stay stuck in self-pity; she spoke life into me when I had none left to speak over myself.

In the quiet moments, when the noise of pain and doubt would settle for just a second, I'd hear it again. That small, persistent voice: *"Trust Me. Step out."*

I was gradually getting better. My body was healing, the pain was still there, but it no longer controlled every part of my day. For the first time in a long time, I could feel strength returning, even if just in small doses. As my recovery continued, the moment I had been dreading started to loom larger: the decision. Would I go back to the job I had spent more than half my life doing, the job that had shaped so much of my routine, my identity, my sense of purpose? Or… would I finally take the step of faith I'd been avoiding for years?

What I didn't realize was that God had already given me the answer. I just hadn't seen it yet.

Before I could return to work, I was required to take a physical test for reentry. I didn't expect it to be easy, but I also didn't expect what came next. After the test results came back, I was officially declared permanently disabled due to the injuries I had sustained. Just like that, the door was closed. I felt defeated.

That job wasn't just work. It was who I was, my rhythm, my title. Without it, I felt like I had lost myself. For a moment, I was completely unmoored, grieving the life I had known, terrified of what came next.

It was a blessing in disguise; I just didn't see it yet. What felt like devastation… was actually divine direction.

Here's the truth: God sees the beginning from the end. He exists outside of time. He knows all things. More importantly… He knows me. Somewhere along the way, I lost sight of that. I stopped leaning on His understanding and started trusting in my own strength, my own timing, my own worth. I thought my work defined me. I thought my effort sustained me. All along, it was the Creator of the universe who had been carrying me, waiting for me to finally let go of my grip and take hold of His.

# Chapter Three

# "Another Door Opens"

With everything I had gone through, every injury, every delay, every moment I felt lost, there was one Scripture I couldn't shake.

**Isaiah 55:8–9**

*"For my thoughts are not your thoughts, neither are your ways my ways, declares the Lord.*

*For as the heavens are higher than the earth, so are my ways higher than your ways and my thoughts than your thoughts."*

Those words became a quiet anthem in my soul. A reminder that even when life didn't make sense to me, it wasn't out of control; it was unfolding exactly as God had planned. I thought the end of my driving career was a loss, but it was a provision in disguise. God had used that very job…the one I thought I'd never escape…to set me up for the next chapter.

Financially, I had what I needed to take a step into the unknown. Emotionally, I had been humbled enough to finally listen. Spiritually, I was in a place of surrender. God closed one door… but He had already built another, and this time, I was ready to walk through it.

In February of 2022, I sat down for my very first real estate class. I felt like a kid again, the excitement, the nerves, the rush of starting something brand new after everything I had been through. It was a feeling I hadn't had in years, the thrill of the unknown, but this time was wrapped in purpose. It wasn't just about learning a new trade, it was about walking in obedience.

For someone who hadn't been in a classroom in years, I was surprised at how natural it felt. I expected to struggle, to feel overwhelmed or out of place, but I didn't. Perhaps it was because everything I was learning was interesting to me. For the first time in a long time, I was hungry to learn. Every slide on the screen, every note I jotted down, all felt like confirmation. You're exactly where you're supposed to be. I didn't feel like I was hustling for survival. I felt like I was building something God had already prepared for me.

Once I completed the course, the next step was preparing for the state license exam. That's when the real studying began. If you're walking this road yourself, let me offer a suggestion: download the **Dearborn Real Estate Exam Prep** app. Yes, it charges a small monthly fee, but in my opinion, it's worth every penny. I genuinely believe that the app played a massive role in helping me pass the exam on my first try. It gave me the confidence and repetition I needed to walk into the testing center with peace of mind.

The day of the exam finally came and let me tell you, I was scared to death. I had studied hard. I had used the app. I had taken the practice tests. But still… walking into that testing center felt like stepping into a courtroom where the verdict was already decided. My hands were sweating. My heart was racing. I had prayed over this moment, asked God for peace, but I still couldn't stop the nerves from creeping in. It wasn't just about passing a test; it was about stepping into a new life…a new calling.

There are two parts to the Exam: General and Law. I had convinced myself that the general portion of the test would be the easy part, that was the stuff that made sense to me. I assumed the law portion would be the one to trip me up. Instead, the general section threw me more curveballs than I expected. Some questions felt familiar, but others made me feel like I had never studied at all. Meanwhile, the law section felt surprisingly clear. I breezed through it faster than I thought I would. It reminded me that sometimes the things we think will be our strengths end up being our biggest lessons.

When I finally hit "submit," my heart stopped. I prayed again, this time a little louder in my head. *"Lord, if this is what You've called me to, I need You to meet me in this moment."* Then I received the results. PASS. I froze for a second, almost unsure if I had read it right. Then it hit me. I had done it. No…we had done it. Me and God. Every step of the way. I stared at the paper for a few more seconds, just to be sure… P-A-S-S!

Those four letters hit me like a wave. I leaned back in the seat of my truck, closed my eyes, and let out a long breath I didn't even know I'd been holding. Then I grabbed my phone. There was only one person I needed to call. My wife. She picked up on the first ring, like she was waiting.

"Well?" she asked, voice hopeful but braced, like she was holding her breath too. I tried to speak, but my throat caught. I had to swallow hard to get the words out.

"I passed," I said. "I actually passed." Silence for a second. Then came the tears: hers and mine.

"I'm so proud of you," she whispered. "I knew you could do it."

Just like that, the weight of the past few years, the doctors' visits, the surgeries, the doubt, the fear, the waiting, all of it broke loose. That phone call was more than just good news, it was a moment of release.

We had been through so much together, and she had seen me at my lowest. She had been my voice of encouragement when I had none. Now, she gets to see me step into the very thing she had prayed for me to do.

As I sat there in my truck after the call, just soaking it all in, a new wave of realization hit me. God hadn't just brought me to this moment; He had shaped me through everything that came before it. Every delay. Every injury. Every time I said "not yet," when I should have said "yes, Lord." Somehow, in His mercy, He used it all.

That's the kind of God He is.

**Romans 8:28** says,

*"And we know that in all things God works for the good of those who love him, who have been called according to his purpose."*

Not some things, not only the good things, ALL things. Broken choices, wasted years, stubborn delays. God didn't abandon me when I ran. He waited. He refined. He worked behind the scenes, turning pain into purpose and delay into development.

Now I could see it clearly I wasn't just becoming a Real Estate Agent, I was becoming the person He had been shaping me into all along. Passing the exam was a huge win, but what came next was a whole new kind of unknown. Now that I was licensed, I had to decide where I would hang that license.

Choosing a brokerage isn't just about picking a company – it's about finding your footing. It's the foundation of your whole career, and back then, I didn't even know what I needed. I was a rookie with a backpack full of knowledge but no map, no compass… just the feeling that I should be moving forward.

I visited a few offices, listened to some pitches, and tried to make sense of all the terms; commission splits, lead systems, desk fees, and mentorship structures. To be honest, I was overwhelmed.

Every Brokerage sounded like they had the answer. Every office seemed to promise success. Deep down, I didn't want hype, I wanted alignment.

I prayed hard during that time:

*"God, place me where I can grow. Not just in business, but in character. Help me find a place that won't just sharpen my skills, but one that will sharpen my spirit too."*

Eventually, I chose a brokerage that didn't just talk numbers; they talked people. They had structure, but more importantly, they had God and mentorship at their foundation. That was exactly what I was really looking for.

I didn't need a flashy brand or the latest tech stack to impress me. What I needed was someone who would walk alongside me while I figured it all out, someone who cared more about who I was becoming than what I was closing.

Funny enough, it turned out they had the trendy brand and the fancy tech. But that wasn't what sold me, it was the sense of alignment. The peace, the feeling that this wasn't just a business decision, this was a God decision.

Something they don't tell you in Real Estate School is that passing the test earns you a license, not a business. I was now an entrepreneur starting from scratch, responsible for building something real and something lasting.

This was paired with no guaranteed paycheck, no boss to follow, and no roadmap. I would have to draw a roadmap with God… in Faith.

Every day felt like jumping into the deep end of the pool without knowing how to swim. But I held tight to what God had already proven to me: If He called me here, He would not leave me here alone. Little by little, the fear began to shrink… and the faith began to grow.

# Chapter Four

# "Mind Set"

I spent 26 years as an employee. Every week, I knew exactly when I would be paid and how much would be deposited into my account. There was structure, security, predictability, and even when I was burnt out or dissatisfied, there was comfort in the rhythm.

So, when I stepped into real estate, I quickly realized I had to unlearn everything I had come to depend on. This new life didn't come with a time clock or a supervisor. Just me – showing up, making plans, pushing forward. Even when the weeks passed without a paycheck. Even when the doubt crept in.

That shift, from employee to entrepreneur, isn't just hard. It's

disorienting. The most challenging part? Letting go of the steady paycheck mindset and stepping into a space where faith and discipline carry more weight than routine.

Here's the truth I had to face:

**When you work a job, you follow someone else's system.**

**When you build a business, you create the system.**

As an employee, I didn't have to wonder where my paycheck was coming from. It was consistent, even when I was disengaged, sick, or just having a bad week. But in real estate? If I didn't work, I didn't eat.

No one was coming to hold me accountable. No one watching over my shoulder. It was up to me to get up, show up, and create momentum every single day. At first, that pressure was terrifying. But over time, I realized: it was also freedom.

I got to decide what kind of business I was going to build.

It was my decision on what values I would stand on. I got to decide whether my success would be driven by desperation or by a calling. So I decided to build something on faith. I wasn't just building a business; I was creating something I wanted God's fingerprints all over.

Colossians 3:23 became my business plan:

*"Whatever you do, work at it with all your heart, as working for the Lord, not for human masters."*

The transition wasn't easy. I stumbled a lot. Every time I showed up when it would've been easier to quit, God met me there. Brick by brick, day by day, I wasn't just making a living, I was building a life I believed in.

If you're considering Real Estate, or you've just stepped into it, here's something I can't stress enough:

**Have money saved before you begin.**

Not "a few bucks for gas and lunch" money. I'm talking about a few months to a year's worth of living expenses. Real Estate takes time to build. There are deals that fall through, buyers who ghost you, and listings that sit for a very long time.

You have to learn how to market yourself, generate leads, and build trust. All of that takes time. It's easy to romanticize the freedom of being your own boss, but freedom without preparation can feel like panic.

Here is a reality check for you:

According to the National Association of Realtors, **87% of new real estate agents leave the industry within the first five years.**

**Eighty-seven percent!**

That number shook me when I first heard it. But after walking through the early stages, I get it. The pressure. The inconsistency. The self-doubt.

But the agents who stay? They learn to think differently. They know that success in this business isn't about clocking in and waiting for a task; it's about waking up every day and deciding to build something. With God's help, that's exactly what I chose to do.

I won't sugarcoat it; those first few weeks and months were tough. Some days, I woke up energized, full of ideas and determination. Other days, I sat in silence, staring at my phone, wondering when the momentum would hit.

Through it all, I kept coming back to a few non-negotiables, habits, and truths that anchored me when the ground felt shaky. Here are a few things that kept me steady as I built my business and my faith muscles at the same time:

## 1. Start the Day With God, Not Your Phone

Before I checked emails, notifications, or the market, I opened my Bible.

Whether it was a full devotional or just a few verses, I needed to align my mind with God's truth before anything else tried to shape it.

One verse that became part of my daily rhythm was:

Proverbs 16:3 –*"Commit to the Lord whatever you do, and He will establish your plans."*

That reminded me: this wasn't just my business…it was His.

## 2. Treat It Like a Job (Because It Is One)

Yes, real estate offers flexibility, but flexibility without discipline can lead to chaos.

I made myself a schedule. I showed up at the same time every morning. I dressed for the day, ready to work, even when there were no appointments on the calendar.

Faith doesn't eliminate structure; it fuels it with purpose.

## 3. Write Down the Wins (Even the Small Ones)

In the early days, a returned phone call or a promising lead was a victory.

I kept a small journal of what I called "God's fingerprints," the little ways He showed up through people, moments, or encouragement when I needed it most.

That journal became a real-time testimony.

## 4. Speak Life Over Your Business

There were days I didn't feel like I was cut out for this.

So I spoke the opposite of what I felt. I'd say things like:

- "God has equipped me for this."
- "The right clients are being prepared for me."
- "My work is ministry and I serve with integrity."

I learned that your mouth will either echo your fear or activate your faith.

**5. Surround Yourself With Encouragers**

Real estate can feel lonely, especially when you're building from scratch.

I leaned on people who believed in me: my wife, my mentors, my church family.

Don't try to go solo when God made you for connection.

These simple practices didn't make everyday easy, but they kept me anchored. I wasn't chasing success anymore. I was walking in obedience and that mindset shift changed everything.

# Chapter Five

# "Faith in the Follow-Up"

If you've ever watched real estate shows on TV, you'd think this business is full of luxury listings, slick negotiations, and instant closings. But real life? It looks a little different. My early days in real estate weren't filled with million-dollar deals or glamorous open houses. They were filled with cold calls, quiet weekdays, a lot of twiddling of my thumbs, and a whole lot of rejection.

I remember sitting at my desk, staring at a list of leads, my heart racing as I dialed each number. The phone felt heavy in my hand. I didn't know what to say after "hello." And when someone actually did pick up? I was so surprised that I stumbled through my script like a kid reading aloud in class. Most of the time, I got voicemail. Other times, I got hung up on.

Then came the open houses. I'd spend hours prepping the space, lighting candles, printing flyers, rehearsing my warm introduction, and then... no one showed up! Not a single visitor. I'd walk through the house alone, praying under my breath: *"Lord, did I miss something? Am I really supposed to be here?"*

Then there were the leads who initially seemed so promising. They were excited, they were ready, they said all the right things, and then… they disappeared. Ghosted. No return texts, no callback, nothing. That kind of silence gets loud after a while, it starts to mess with your confidence, it makes you question your calling.

Through that I learned Real Estate, like faith, is about planting seeds you may not see grow right away. Every call, every follow-up, every open house that felt like a waste of time was all part of the process.

**Galatians 6:9** became my reminder: *"Let us not grow weary in doing good, for at the proper time we will reap a harvest if we do not give up."*

That verse kept me going. Because while it didn't always feel like I was building something… I was. One conversation at a time, one showing at a time, and one faithful step at a time. Even when nobody else saw it yet, God did.

My advice? Wherever you are, don't be afraid to share what you do. Whether you're at the grocery store, waiting at the dentist, or chatting with someone after church, simple conversations can open unexpected doors. Time and time again, I've picked up new clients just by mentioning that I'm a Realtor. Nothing salesy, nothing forced just simply being genuine, friendly, and transparent, and letting people know what I do.

You wouldn't believe how many times I've heard something like, *"Wow, that's crazy, we were just talking about finding a Realtor yesterday."* That's not coincidence. That's opportunity meeting obedience.

If God called you into this work, then wherever you go, so does your purpose. Don't shrink back, don't play small. You never know who's waiting for exactly what you carry.

Here's a real-life example of how simply letting people know what you do can bring significant rewards.

My wife and I were in a local tea shop, grabbing one of her favorite drinks. While we were waiting in line, we struck up a conversation with a couple of other customers. My wife introduced herself, and when it was my turn, I added, "I'm a Realtor." Instantly, they looked at each other in surprise. *"That's crazy,"* one of them said. *"We're looking for a Realtor right now."*

It turns out that I had already placed business cards at that shop a while back. I reached behind them, grabbed one, and handed it to them with a smile. That small gesture not only gave them my contact info, but it also added a layer of legitimacy, proof that I wasn't just talking the talk.

Months passed. Then one day, I got the call: *"We're ready to start looking!"*

After a thorough search and numerous showings, I helped them find their forever home. It was one of the most rewarding transactions I've had, because it wasn't just a sale. It was a relationship that started with a simple conversation.

**The point?** If I hadn't spoken up, if I had kept quiet about what I do, they never would have known. And they likely would have worked with someone else.

That moment reminded me: **God will bring opportunity but we still have to open our mouths.**

Do not underestimate the power of being visible in your calling. Whether you're in a tea shop or a church lobby, your obedience can turn a casual encounter into a life-changing connection for them and for you.

That experience reminded me of something deeper than just business: **Blessings often follow boldness.**

When I first started in Real Estate, I was hesitant to tell people what I did for a living.

Not because I was ashamed, but because I didn't feel established yet. I worried that if they asked questions I couldn't answer, I'd be exposed as "new" or inexperienced.

But what I've learned is this:

**God doesn't wait for us to be polished before He starts using us.**

He just asks us to show up as ourselves, with courage and authenticity. Being bold in my identity as a Realtor, and even more so as a Man of God in this field, has led to unexpected blessings.

Clients who turned into friends. Deals I didn't see coming.

Conversations that started casually and ended with someone saying, "I really needed that today." I've come to realize that boldness isn't about confidence in myself. It's about confidence in who sent me.

**Proverbs 28:1** says, *"The righteous are as bold as a lion."*

That doesn't mean arrogant. That means **anchored.** When you know who you are and, more importantly, Whose you are, you can walk into any room, any conversation, any opportunity, knowing that you're not alone.

So, if you're reading this and feeling timid about sharing your calling, don't be. You never know what God will do with your courage. You're not selling yourself. You're standing in the purpose He's already prepared for you.

### Marketing vs. Ministry

In real estate, you're taught early on that you need to market yourself. You need a brand, a slogan, a headshot, a presence. None of that is wrong, in fact, it's necessary. You can't help people if they don't know who you are.

**Marketing is about visibility. Ministry is about availability.**

Marketing says, *"Look at me."* Ministry says, *"How can I serve you?"* One promotes a product. The other offers presence.

As a Realtor, I utilize social media, hand out business cards, and network because visibility is crucial. But I constantly ask myself this question: *"Am I pointing people toward my service or toward the God who called me to serve?"*

When I shift from marketing to ministry, everything changes.

·  A showing becomes a chance to listen.

·  A deal becomes a moment to build trust.

·  A closing becomes a celebration of God's provision, not just my success.

I'm not just trying to win clients, I'm trying to leave people better than I found them, even if we never work together.

I do this because I don't represent a company… **I represent the Kingdom.** When your business becomes a ministry, you stop worrying about who's ahead of you or what you're missing, and you start trusting that **God will bring the right people to your door at the right time.** It doesn't mean you won't work hard, it just means you'll work in peace.

**Colossians 3:17** puts it this way: *"Whatever you do, whether in word or deed, do it all in the name of the Lord Jesus…"*

If you keep this mindset, you won't just build a successful career, you'll create a business that reflects the very heart of God. I've learned that in this business, success isn't just about the number of closings you have, it's about how many people you serve well.

Early on, I made a decision:

I didn't want to be just another agent. I wanted to be God's representative in every transaction.

**That meant:**

· bringing integrity to the table, even when it costs me.

· being patient when a client was difficult or fearful.

· listening not just to what they said, but to what the Holy Spirit might be saying in the moment.

· Sometimes pausing a deal.

· Sometimes praying silently in my car before a showing.

· Sometimes just showing up with peace when everyone else was stressed.


Each time I leaned into <u>serving</u> instead of selling, I could feel God's presence in the process. It reminded me that this isn't just a business, it's a ministry.

When you ask God to lead, He will. And when you serve people with His heart, you don't just build a reputation, you build relationships that last.

# Chapter Six

# "Plant the Seeds"

Faith and routine go hand in hand. You can believe in big promises from God but if you're not showing up every day to prepare the ground, you'll never see the harvest.

One of the greatest lessons I've learned is this:

God honors consistency, not perfection or the hustle for the sake of the hustle. Instead, steady and faithful effort done in obedience to His will.

In the early months of real estate, it felt like I was working and working with little to no result. I wasn't seeing fruit, I wasn't getting calls back and the deals weren't closing.

But I kept hearing this in my spirit: *"Keep planting."*

Just like a farmer doesn't see a harvest the same day he puts seeds in the ground, neither do we. That's why routine is so important. Even when you don't see results, your daily actions matter. They're creating momentum, building trust, shaping your character, and aligning you for what's to come.

**Daily Disciplines That Build Your Faith and Your Business**

**1. Start the Day With God**

Before emails, before texts, before the day hijacks your peace, spend time with the One who called you. Read a chapter of Proverbs. Pray over your schedule. Ask God to guide your conversations.

**Matthew 6:33** - *"Seek first the Kingdom…"* This isn't just spiritual, it's strategic.

**2. Set a Simple, Sustainable Schedule**

You don't need a 47-step productivity system, you need a rhythm. Time block for lead generation. Schedule follow-ups. Plan breaks. Be intentional, but realistic.

Faith isn't just about believing God will show up, it's about preparing for when He does.

**3. Reach Out Every Day (Even When You Don't Feel Like It)**

I challenged myself to reach out to at least five people every weekday, whether through calls, texts, check-ins, or past clients and prospects.

It didn't always lead to business. But it kept the soil of connection fertile.

**Galatians 6:9** - *"Let us not grow weary in doing good…"*

**4. God's Provision**

I started writing down "God moments" in my business: a kind word, a client referral, a prayer answered.

On the hard days, I'd go back and read those pages. They reminded me: He's moving, even when I don't see it yet.

Planting seeds is about believing before you see the results. You won't always see the fruit right away, but God is not blind to your obedience. When you show up daily, with a heart that's open and hands that are willing, He brings the increase.

**1 Corinthians 3:6** says,

*"I planted the seed, Apollos watered it, but God has been making it grow."*

That's how business in the Kingdom works.

You plant.

You water.

And He brings the harvest.

My first official day as a licensed Real Estate Agent didn't come with confetti, balloons, or a crowd of cheering clients. It was quiet, simple, and yet, it felt monumental.

I woke up early that morning with a strange mix of emotions: part anticipation, part fear, part awe. I stood in front of the mirror and said out loud:

"You're really doing this."

This wasn't just a new career; this was a new identity, a new

beginning. After spending decades in a uniform, following someone else's schedule, clocking in and out of a life I no longer felt called to… this moment felt surreal.

I didn't have all the answers. I didn't know where my first client would come from. I didn't know how to build a brand or compete with agents who had been in the business for years. What I did know was I had something stronger than certainty. I had a calling.

I had the kind of peace that only comes when you're finally doing what you were meant to do.

**Proverbs 16:9** says, *"In their hearts humans plan their course, but the Lord establishes their steps."*

That day, I didn't know what each step would look like, but I knew who was guiding me. I walked into the office that morning like a Freshman on the first day of school. I smiled, nodded, and pretended like I wasn't overwhelmed, but inside, I was asking God to steady my hands and quiet my nerves.

I didn't have a full pipeline or a long list of leads. I had faith, I had the willingness, and I had a why. Sometimes, that's exactly what God needs to do something extraordinary.

My executive broker wasn't just someone who handed me a desk and wished me luck; she was someone whose life and leadership reflected the heart of God. A woman who had overcome more obstacles than most people can imagine. Her strength didn't come from titles or accolades; it came from a deep well of humility and faith. She carried herself with quiet confidence, the kind that didn't demand attention but commanded respect.

What struck me most wasn't just her business insight or industry experience; it was her desire to grow the Kingdom, not just the company. She led with prayer, spoke life, and empowered those around her, not just to sell homes, but to build something eternal. I watched her pour wisdom into agents just getting started, guiding them to build businesses with character, clarity, and conviction. She taught us to lead with service, to prioritize people over profit, and to invite God into every deal, conversation, and decision.

Her influence reminded me that success doesn't require sacrificing your soul. Instead, leadership rooted in Christ can transform not just a team, but an entire culture. I didn't just find a broker, I found a leader, a teacher, a woman of God who was walking her calling and calling others up in the process.

What she may not have fully seen and would never boast about, was that with every word of encouragement, every prayer over an agent, every example of integrity in action, she was planting seeds.

Seeds led by God, intended for transformation in hearts and my heart was changing.

## Alignment Matters: The Right Brokerage, The Right Leadership

One of the most important decisions I made early in my real estate journey, though I didn't fully realize it at the time, was choosing the right brokerage. Most people think about branding, fees, splits, tech, and leads, those things do matter. But for me, I was seeking something more profound.

I needed to be in an environment where my faith didn't just "fit in"…it flourished.

God knew what I needed before my license was in hand.

Not only did I have an excellent Executive Broker, a woman of wisdom, grace, and fierce spiritual leadership, but I was also blessed to align under a Principal Broker with a Kingdom-first mindset.

He wasn't just running a business. He was building a culture. A culture where integrity came before income, where service came before success, and where God came before growth. He poured wisdom into me from years in the field, but more than that, he led with conviction. He reminded me that real estate can be done with excellence and character. That faith doesn't have to stay outside the office door. That you can be competitive without compromising who you are in Christ.

Both of these leaders... helped shape me into the Realtor I am today. They didn't just teach contracts and compliance. They taught a calling. So if you're reading this as a new or aspiring agent, let me say this as clearly as I can: **Align with people who align with your values, because the right brokerage won't just help you grow your business. They'll help you grow your purpose.**

# Chapter Seven

# "First Fruit of the Calling"

"I want you to be my agent." Nothing prepares you for the first time you hear that. You study, train, role-play scripts, sit through seminars about negotiations, contracts, and fiduciary duty. But the first time a real person, with real needs, real money, and real dreams trusts you to guide them through one of the most significant decisions of their life, it hits differently.

I remember the call. The phone rang, I answered. My heart jumped. I tried to stay calm, to sound professional and confident, but inside I was freaking out. Suddenly, all the nerves and "what ifs" came flooding in: *What if I mess this up? What if I forget something important? What if I'm not really ready?* Then I remembered: *I didn't get here by accident, and I'm not walking into this alone.* Everything slowed down and the call went well and we scheduled a time to meet.

I prayed before I met with them, not just for the deal, but for everyone involved. *"God, help me to serve them well. Help me to listen. Help me to guide them with integrity. Let this be about more than a closing."*

When we sat down face-to-face, I saw it in their eyes: uncertainty, hope, fear, excitement - all of it. I realized something profound: They were feeling the same way I was.

That moment became more than a first deal. It became the moment I truly understood what it meant to represent someone. It wasn't just about signing papers or finding the right property. It was about being a source of peace in the process. A guide. A steady hand. A reflection of God's character in the middle of something stressful.

**Colossians 3:23** says,

*"Whatever you do, work at it with all your heart, as working for the Lord, not for human masters."*

That Scripture took on new meaning for me. This wasn't just about doing a good job, it was about serving people in a way that honored God. Representing someone for the first time taught me that real estate is more than sales. It's stewardship. That calling… felt holy.

As it turns out, my very first transaction wasn't with a stranger. It was with my son and his wife. This made it even more special and more terrifying.

On one hand, it was an incredible honor. There's something sacred about helping your own child take a significant step into their future. I didn't just witness it; I was an actual part of it. I was able to serve them, advise them, pray for them, and celebrate with them.

On the other hand, it also added an entirely new level of pressure. This wasn't just a "transaction," this was family. My kid, my legacy. I didn't want to miss a detail, I didn't want to come up short. I felt the weight of making sure everything was done with excellence and care.

There were a few moments where I second-guessed myself. Did I explain that clearly enough? Should I double-check that contract again? Am I really equipped to do this?

In those moments of anxiety, I reminded myself of the same truth I'd clung to throughout this journey: God called me to this, and if He called me, He would also equip me.

I took my time, asked questions when I needed to, and prayed before every step. I reminded myself this wasn't about being perfect, it was about being faithful.

When closing day finally came, I watched my son and daughter-in-law sign the last of the papers, smiles on their faces, keys in hand, and I felt it. That overwhelming, quiet, joyful moment of purpose fulfilled. I wasn't just handing over keys. I was handing them a future. And it was only the beginning.

Looking back, I learned more in this first transaction than any course, podcast, or seminar could have taught me. Representing my son and daughter-in-law added emotional weight.

Here are a few takeaways that helped shape how I approach every client now:

### 1. Treat Every Client Like They're Family, But Don't Cut Corners If They Are

Even though I was working with my son, I didn't skip a step. I followed the entire process, triple-checked the paperwork, and remained professional in every interaction. When working with people you know, it's tempting to "relax" the formalities. Don't. Treat family and friends with the same excellence you'd give a stranger, they're trusting you with a major life decision.

### 2. Stay Humble, Stay Teachable

No matter how well you've studied, your first transaction will reveal what you don't know. Be willing to ask your broker or mentor questions. Admit when you need help. Don't fake confidence, build it through humility and preparation.

### 3. Overcommunicate

Clients, especially first-time buyers, need reassurance. They may not always know what to ask, so take the initiative to explain the next steps clearly. Regular updates, check-ins, and transparency build trust. I made a point to touch base with my clients (even my family) consistently, and they appreciated the professionalism.

### 4.  Stay Organized

Between contracts, disclosures, timelines, inspections, and lender communication, it's easy to get overwhelmed. Use a checklist or transaction management system, even a simple spreadsheet, to help you stay organized. Disorganization can cost time, money, and credibility.

### 5.Pray Over Every Deal

Even in the business world, prayer has a place. I prayed before showings, before phone calls, and definitely before closing day. Prayer helped settle my nerves and reminded me that I wasn't in this alone. God cares about how you serve people; He's in the details, too.

Your first transaction will stretch you. It may challenge your confidence. It may expose some blind spots. But it will also confirm your calling. Don't aim for perfection, strive for faithfulness, serve with integrity, ask questions, stay humble, and trust God to fill in the gaps.

# Chapter Eight

# "Baptism by Fire"

My first non-family transaction was, without a doubt, one of the most challenging I've ever encountered. It wasn't a sweet couple buying their first home. It wasn't someone from my church or an old friend who automatically trusted me. No, this one was a foreclosure. Not just any foreclosure, but the kind that comes with its own maze of red tape, bank requirements, deadlines, delays, and enough paperwork to make your head spin.

The client? A guy I'd never met before, who found me on Yelp. Yelp. Of all places.

To this day, I sometimes wonder if he meant to click on someone else's profile. But for whatever reason, call it divine appointment or just online luck, he called me. He was ready. He had the address, the lender's pre-approval, and his eye on that foreclosed property as if it were gold.

What he didn't have... Any idea that I was brand new.

I answered the phone with my "professional voice," took down the info, and calmly said, "Great, I'll get to work on this and follow up soon." Then I hung up and panicked. I started Googling every word I didn't fully understand. I called my broker. I looked for every article, checklist, and prayer I could find about how to handle a foreclosure deal.

"Might as well get the hard one out of the way upfront," my wife told me with a grin. I laughed nervously. She wasn't wrong.

Without going through every painful twist and turn, I'll say this: a foreclosure isn't difficult… if you know what you're doing. I didn't.

But I showed up. I learned on the fly. I asked for help. I made notes on everything. I prayed a lot. Somehow, despite all my inexperience, the deal made it to the finish line. The client never knew just how green I was, though I'm sure he had his suspicions.

That transaction taught me one of the most valuable lessons of all:

**You don't have to be perfect. You just have to be present.**

God doesn't always start us with the easy wins sometimes He throws us into the deep end, not to drown us, but to teach us how to swim.

Looking back, I'm glad that deal was hard. It humbled me, stretched me, and made the next one feel a little less scary. Most importantly, it reminded me that success in real estate and life isn't about having it all figured out.

**It's about trusting the One who does.**

After that transaction, I realized something.

*I couldn't just rely on knowledge.*

*I couldn't just hustle harder.*

*I needed to invite God into every deal.*

So I started praying for my clients I prayed before we even met, before the showings, before the offers, before the signatures. "God, help me serve this person with excellence. Give me wisdom. Give me peace. Let me be a calm presence in their process." Some of my clients were believers, some weren't. It didn't matter. The prayers weren't for show. They were for alignment. Real Estate is full of pressure – money, timing, emotion, and conflict. When I prayed, I was reminded of something bigger than the deal, the person behind it.

I also had to learn to set boundaries, something I wasn't very good at initially.

When you're new, you feel like you have to say yes to everything. You're afraid that if you don't jump the second someone needs you, you'll lose the client. Answering every call, text, no matter the day or time. But I started to feel convicted. How could I be present with my family, worship, or rest…if I never unplug and recharge. So I began to stop working on Sundays and I stopped taking non-urgent calls during dinner. I reminded myself, I work hard, but God provides. And surprisingly, I didn't lose business. I gained clarity and peace.

Then there were the tough deals, the ones where clients got angry, emotions ran high, or I was pressured to cut corners to make something work.

In those moments, I had to decide; was I just an Agent or was I a believer who happened to be an Agent? There's a difference.

**Integrity isn't always convenient. It doesn't always feel "business smart." But it is Kingdom smart.**

I learned to walk away from opportunities that didn't align with my values. I learned to speak truth with grace, even when it was uncomfortable. I knew that honoring God in the deal sometimes means letting go of the deal.

Every time I chose faith over fear, God made a way. Real estate taught me how to trust God in the practical. Not just in church. Not just when I'm reading Scripture.

Trust in the offer.

Trust in the inspection.

Trust in the negotiation.

Trust in the silence between deals.

And through it all, I've realized something powerful: This career isn't just my calling…it's my ministry.

# Chapter Nine

## "Faithful in the Slow Season"

Slow seasons are part of the job. This was very hard to learn.

The leads dry up.

The listings disappear.

Deals fall through.

Suddenly, the momentum you felt when you first got started comes to a screeching halt. It's in those quiet, uncertain moments that doubt begins to whisper. *"Maybe this isn't for you." "Maybe you missed it." "Maybe God's not in this after all."*

It's easy to trust God when the closings are consistent, the pipeline is full, and the referrals keep coming in. Can you trust Him when it's just you, your thoughts, and a blank calendar? Can you stay faithful when the fruit isn't immediate? Can you show up, pray up, and keep working even when it feels like nothing's moving? In those slow seasons, I've learned that God is often doing His best work, not around me, but in me.

- He's refining my motives.

- He's testing my trust.

- He's reminding me that this business doesn't rise and fall with market trends, it rises and falls with my obedience.

**Galatians 6:9 says:**

*"Let us not become weary in doing good, for at the proper time we will reap a harvest if we do not give up."*

That verse has carried me through more than one slow season. It's a reminder that the harvest will come but only if I don't give up in the meantime.

So what do I do when things slow down? I get back to basics.

- I pray.
- I follow up.
- I sow seeds I may not see grow for months.
- I check in on past clients, not to get something, but to bless them.
- I keep my routine. I keep my integrity. I keep my peace.
- I worship.

**Sometimes, worship is the most powerful weapon you have when the world says,** *"You should be panicking."*

The slow season isn't a curse. It's part of the process. It's where God asks, *"Do you trust Me, or do you only trust results?"* The world tells us to measure success by numbers. The Kingdom measures success by faithfulness, so I've made a decision:

Whether the season is full or empty, fast or slow. I will remain faithful, because I know who planted me. I know what He promised.

## When Faith Had to Be Enough

Recently, the market took a hard downturn. Interest rates rose, buyer confidence dropped, and everything slowed to a crawl. I had months with no closings, no new leads, and nothing in the pipeline. And the bills? They didn't get the memo. They kept stacking up, just like the pressure. I found myself staring at the ceiling some nights, wondering, *When will I be paid again?* I had done the work, followed up, and shown up. But the harvest wasn't showing up, yet.

It takes faith not to panic. It takes faith to say, *"God, You brought me here, and You didn't bring me here to leave me."*

One morning, during a quiet time of prayer, I read this verse, and it felt like a lifeline:

### Matthew 6:26

*"Look at the birds of the air; they do not sow or reap or store away in barns, and yet your heavenly Father feeds them. Are you not much more valuable than they?"*

That hit me like a fresh wind. If God feeds the birds, who don't stress, don't hustle, don't panic… surely He would take care of me.

Then… it happened. Deals started to come in from nowhere. Not from all the leads I had been chasing. Not from the emails or the cold calls.

A past client referred a friend out of the blue. Someone I hadn't talked to in months called, ready to list. A family member of a contact I almost forgot about needed help buying a home. Deal after deal showed up, miraculously, right when I needed them most. All I could do was shake my head, lift my hands, and say: *"You are faithful, God. Always."*

I still believe in hard work, lead generation, follow-ups, and systems. But more than anything, I believe in this: **God is my Provider.**

This slow season taught me to trust Him deeper. Not because of what I see in the bank account… But because I know who holds my future. And that's more than enough.

# Chapter Ten

# "Obedience Leads to Overflow"

When I first entered the real estate industry, I thought I was answering a call to a new career. I had no idea I was stepping into a whole new season of purpose. I thought I was walking through just one open door but God was setting me up to walk through many.

Within my first two years as a Realtor, something unexpected began to happen. I started to see the business in a different light. Not just from the lens of buying and selling for clients… but as a path to build something of my own… something lasting. That's when the idea of real estate investing took root.

The deeper I got into the industry, the more opportunities I saw all around me: homes that were undervalued, listings that needed work, and properties that other buyers overlooked.

Being a Realtor gave me the edge. I knew how to run comps. I understood the paperwork. I had access to properties the minute they hit the market. Most importantly, I was walking in obedience so I had discernment that only comes from the Holy Spirit.

One day I came across a small, overlooked home in need of some love. Most people would've passed it up. In fact, most people did. It wasn't flashy or in perfect shape, but something about it stood out to me. I ran the numbers, prayed, asked for wisdom, and spoke with my wife. Then we pulled the trigger.

That under loved home became our first rental property! The first home we bought, fixed up, and turned into a steady stream of income. I didn't have a fancy investment strategy. I had faith, a little knowledge, and a willingness to move when God said move.

That one deal sparked something inside me. It showed me that God's provision didn't stop with a career change. He was giving me a vision for legacy. For income streams that didn't just pay today's bills, but could create freedom for tomorrow. It all started because I said yes to the first door He opened.

That's the thing about obedience. It doesn't always lead you to one blessing. Sometimes, it positions you for multiple streams of blessing, streams you couldn't have imagined on your own.

## The First Investment

I found my first rental property the same way I'd found homes for clients on the MLS. There was nothing flashy about the listing, no "hot deal" flags, or all caps headlines screaming opportunity, but when I saw it, I knew.

It was tucked in a neighborhood most investors weren't even looking. It needed serious work. The roof was a mess from a fallen tree, the floors were uneven, and it had that "hasn't been touched in decades" kind of feel. I ran the numbers and more importantly I prayed. The numbers showed it *could* work and God gave me peace that it *would.*

I used cash to purchase the home outright, something I had never imagined doing even a couple of years earlier. It was a stretch, but I knew the equity would give me options.

After the purchase, I refinanced the property using a construction loan to fund the remodel. That's when things got real.

I didn't hire a full crew. I didn't have a general contractor running the show. I was the crew most of the time. There were days I came home covered in dust, sore from head to toe, questioning whether I'd made the right call. Days when things didn't go as planned, when materials were backordered, when the timeline stretched longer than expected. But I kept showing up because this wasn't just about fixing a house. It was about building something with God.

Every swing of the hammer, every late-night paint job, every trip to the hardware store, it all felt like part of a bigger picture. I'd listen to worship music as I worked. I'd pray in the rooms as I restored them. And I started to realize… This house was a metaphor for me. Worn out in some places, needing repair in others, but still valuable, still capable of being made new.

When the remodel was done and the property was rented, I didn't just feel proud, I felt grateful. Grateful for the sweat. Grateful for the help. Grateful for the slow days. Grateful that God had taught me not just how to invest, but how to build. Now, that property provides consistent income, not just from an investment, but from obedience and faith in motion.

# Chapter Eleven

# "Building for More Than Me"

There was a moment after finishing my first rental, standing in that empty living room, freshly painted and ready for tenants, when it hit me: *This isn't just for me.*

It wasn't just about closing another deal or earning another stream of income. It was about what I was building and who I was building it for.

For so many years, I was focused on getting by, paying the bills, and surviving the season I was in. Now, for the first time, I was thinking long-term. Legacy, faith, freedom, and not just mine, but my family's as well.

I want to give my kids and grandkids something more than a strong work ethic. I want to provide them with a foundation of faith, a vision for ownership, a model of what it looks like to honor God in business.

I want them to know that wealth is a tool, not a god. That success is a gift, not a requirement, and that freedom isn't just about having money. It's about having options that are aligned with purpose.

Real Estate has given me a platform to think bigger. I now see each investment property as a seed. Something I can pass on, something my grandkids can learn from, something that could fund ministry, support missions, or give them the chance to chase their own God-given dreams without being chained to a paycheck.

**Proverbs 13:22** says,

*"A good person leaves an inheritance for their children's children…"*

Inheritance isn't just about money. It's about values passed down, vision lived out, and a legacy that outlives us.

I want to build a name in Real Estate… but I want my family name to carry more weight in the Kingdom than on any sign or business card.

So, I'm no longer building just for profit. I'm building for impact, faith, for the next generation, and for the glory of the One who opened every door I've walked through.

## What I'd Tell the Old Me

If I could sit across the table from the guy I used to be… The one working long hours with a sore back and a full heart, but no clear direction… The one afraid to make the leap, worried about money, timing, and whether or not he was really "called"… I'd tell him this:

"You have no idea how faithful God is about to be. The fear won't last forever, but the impact will. You're not just changing careers, you're stepping into a calling. Obedience won't always be easy, but it will always be worth it. God doesn't need you to be perfect, just willing." I'd tell him that the late nights, the slow seasons, the scary first steps… they'll turn into something beautiful. I'd say to him "you're not building a business, you're building a legacy: one closing, one client, one prayer at a time."

Then I'd tell him something I hope you hear too, if you're just starting out:

- Trust God more than the market.
- Serve people before you sell to them.
- Don't chase every opportunity, pray about which ones you're meant to walk through.
- Don't compare your journey to anyone else's; this is between you and the One who called you.
- Never forget: the slow days, the quiet months, the moments you wonder if this is really working, those are the very moments where your faith is being forged.

So keep showing up, keep learning, keep walking in obedience even if you're walking in uncertainty. Because one day, you'll look back and see that every hard moment was part of the foundation God was laying. You'll realize: **He was building something greater than you imagined.**

# Chapter Twelve

# "What the First Year Actually Looks Like"

When people think of becoming a Realtor, they usually picture the highlight reel: nice cars, flexible schedules, big commission checks, and maybe even a feature on HGTV. What they don't often see is the hard truth about the first year: It's tough, it's emotional, and for most, it's financially humbling.

As I stated in an earlier chapter, according to the National Association of Realtors (NAR), **nearly 87% of real estate agents fail within the first five years.** Many don't even make it past their first year. The dream is real, and so is the grind.

### The Reality of Year One

Let's start with some numbers:

· Average first-year income: Around $8,000 to $12,000, depending on your market, many make less.

· Average time to first closing: Typically 90–120 days, sometimes longer.

· Out-of-pocket expenses: You can expect to spend anywhere from \$3,000 to \$10,000 in your first year between licensing, dues, marketing, gas, signs, continuing education, and tools.

· Hours worked per week: Most successful new agents work 40-60+ hours a week getting started.

Now here's the truth they won't always tell you in training: you might work for weeks or months before you see your first paycheck. That can do a number on your confidence if you're not prepared for it mentally, spiritually, and financially.

### My First Year Snapshot

When I got my license, I was excited, fired up, and called. I had the support of my wife, a great brokerage, and faith that God was in it. Still, it wasn't easy.

My first client was a family member, which gave me a head start. After that, I had to hustle for every lead. I spent hours learning contracts, practicing scripts, researching listings, showing homes, and trying to keep my faith steady when my pipeline was dry.

There were moments of doubt, where I wondered if I'd made the right decision. There were days I felt like giving up. Yet, God kept whispering, "Keep going. I called you to this."

My first year taught me endurance to celebrate the small wins and to rely on God, not just on my own efforts.

### Faith Over Fear

There's a spiritual weight to starting over, especially later in life or after a career shift. I wasn't just launching a business, I was rebuilding my identity. Through it all, I learned that **faithfulness beats fruitfulness** in the early seasons. Results will come, your job is to show up with excellence and integrity every single day.

**Hebrews 10:35–36** says, *"So do not throw away your confidence; it will be richly rewarded. You need to persevere so that when you have done the will of God, you will receive what he has promised."*

If you're stepping into real estate, expect the grind. Don't fear it, embrace it and remember: God doesn't call us to comfort; He calls us to grow.

Your first year may not look glamorous, but it can be the year your faith grows stronger than your fear. The year you learn what it means to walk in obedience, even when you don't see the results yet.

You're not just building a career, you're building character and if you stay faithful the fruit will follow.

# Chapter Thirteen

# "Your First 100 Days: Strategy, Systems, and Sanity"

The first 100 days as a Realtor can make or break you. This is where routines are built, habits are formed, and mindsets are either strengthened or sabotaged. The goal in these early days isn't perfection, it's traction.

Think of your first 100 days like building a foundation. You may not see the fruit yet, but you're laying the bricks that will support your future success.

### Structure Your Time Like You Mean It

Treat your new business like a job, even if you're not getting paid yet. Set office hours, wake up early, dress like you're going to appointments. Show up mentally and spiritually ready.

**Suggested Daily Framework:**

7:00am – Devotion/prayer time

8:00am – Review MLS, market updates

9:00am – Lead generation (calls, texts, social media)

12:00pm – Lunch/networking

1:00pm – Client appointments/showings

4:00pm – Training or skill-building

6:00pm – Family time / wind down

## Learn Before You Need It

Don't wait until you have a client to learn how to write a contract. Don't wait until a deal falls apart to understand contingencies.

**Use your first 100 days to:**

- Practice writing offers
- Review sample inspection reports
- Shadow experienced agents
- Watch training videos on disclosures, timelines, and negotiations

**Pro tip:** Join every training your brokerage offers, show up early, ask questions, and be teachable.

## Build a System Before You Build a Brand

Everyone wants the fancy logos, the Instagram aesthetic, and the slick business cards. That's branding. However, if you don't have systems in place to support the leads and clients you're praying for, you won't retain them.

**Start with these systems:**

- A simple CRM software (Customer Relationship Management) or even a spreadsheet works at first
- A daily follow-up routine
- Templates for email/text responses
- A clear process from first contact to post-closing

### Start Conversations, Not Just Marketing

In your first 100 days, aim to talk to at least 5-10 people every day about real estate. Not a sales pitch, just a conversation.

· "Hey! I just got into real estate. If you or someone you know is thinking about buying or selling, I'd love to be chat with them!"

· "Do you know what your home is worth in today's market?"

Your goal isn't to be pushy, it's to be present.

### Stay Spiritually Anchored

The first 100 days are exciting, but also exhausting. That's why spiritual routine is just as vital as your work routine.

· Start your day with prayer.

· Speak God's promises over your goals.

· Worship through the waiting.

**Psalm 90:17** says, *"Let the favor of the Lord our God be upon us, and establish the work of our hands."*

Ask for God's favor, not just for success, but for impact. Let Him establish your work. You won't have it all figured out in your first 100 days. You will be building momentum, and be learning how to work smart and serve well. You'll be laying the groundwork not just for transactions, but for transformation.

You've got the license, the calling, now build the habits that will carry the mission.

# Chapter Fourteen

# "The Real Costs of Being a Realtor"

There's more to starting a real estate career than getting your license and posting a headshot online. Many new agents underestimate the high cost of launching and sustaining a business in this industry. If you're not financially prepared, the first year can break you, not because you're unskilled, but because you run out of resources.

### Start-Up Costs

Here's a basic breakdown of typical first-year costs (varies by market and brokerage):

- Licensing course & exam: $300–$800
- State application & background check: $100–$200
- MLS access & association dues: $500–$1,200 annually
- Brokerage fees: $50–$500/month (or a commission split of 15%–40%)
- Supra lockbox/key fees: $100–$300/year
- Business cards, signage, marketing materials: $200–$1,000+
- Website or CRM subscriptions: $30–$100/month
- Continuing education: $100–$300/year

·    Fuel, meals, client gifts, showing supplies: Costs, can easily be $200-$500/month

**According to the National Association of Realtors (NAR):**

- The median income for new agents (less than 2 years of experience) is $9,600/year.

- 50% of new agents earn less than $10,000 in their first year.

- Only 13% of all Realtors make over $100,000/year.

- Most new agents don't see a consistent income until year 2 or 3.

**Hidden Costs Most New Agents Forget**

- Your time. You'll be working unpaid for months. That has a cost.

- Health insurance and retirement. You're now self-employed, there's no 401(k) match or company healthcare.

- Tax prep. You'll need to set aside 20-30% of your income for taxes and possibly hire a CPA.

- Downtime between closings. Commissions don't arrive until the deal closes. You could go months without a paycheck.

**How I Managed It**

When I started, I was blessed to have some savings from my previous career. Even then, the budget was tight. I treated every dollar like a seed… prayed over it, budgeted it, and invested wisely. I didn't go out and buy fancy branding right away. I waited to spend until I had some income coming in. I tracked every expense and tithed from my very first commission. Even when it was tough, I trusted God with my finances.

**Luke 16:10** says, *"Whoever can be trusted with very little can also be trusted with much."*

I wanted to prove faithful in the little so that God could increase my capacity over time.

### Tips for Financial Survival and Stewardship

- Build a 6–12 month reserve.

- Create a monthly budget for both business and personal expenses.

- Separate your business and personal accounts early on.

- Track your miles and expenses, don't leave money on the table come tax time.

- Tithe and give even when it's small. It keeps your heart in the right place.

Being a Realtor is expensive up front. But that cost is an investment in your calling. It's not just about getting rich; it's about building something sustainable, God-honoring, and deeply impactful. Don't fear the cost, prepare for it. Trust that when God calls you, He will also equip you. Where He guides, He provides.

# Chapter Fifteen

# "Powerful Prospecting Activities"

If you're just starting out in real estate, here's one truth you'll quickly discover: your success isn't just about how well you understand contracts or know the market, it's about how many people you connect with. That all begins with **prospecting**.

In this chapter, we're going to break down powerful, practical ways to grow your database, generate leads, and plant the seeds for long-term success. These aren't gimmicks, they're real activities used by successful agents who started exactly where you are right now.

You don't need to be a natural-born salesperson. You just need to be consistent, authentic, and open to trying new things. Your next client is out there and by the end of this chapter, you'll have multiple ways to find them.

Let's dive in and start filling your pipeline, one powerful prospecting activity at a time.

1. Open Houses

2. Floor Duty at your brokerage

3. Door Knocking

4. Direct mail

5. Pop by's (Stop by a businesses or to see an individual)

6. E-Newsletters

7. Phone Calls

8. For Sale By Owners (Do a complimentary home evaluation)

9. Face-to-face meetings and appointments

10. Expired or Withdrawn Listings (I picked up my first few listings this way)

11. Client Appreciation Party

12. Volunteer for community events

13. Networking Events

14. Coach your kid's sports team

15. Create a Comparative Market Analysis for prospective clients

16. Circle prospecting

17. Post cards

18. Shake hands with a stranger and give them your business card

19. Email drip campaigns

20. REO/HUD/Bank Listings

21. Attend public sales

22. Trade shows/ Home shows

23. Host an informational seminar/ talk

24. Put your nametag or Logo on and attend an event

25. Enroll in a class or a new hobby to meet people

26. Join a book club

27. Target renters

28. Mail home anniversary cards

29. Create and hand out a personal brochure

30. Radio campaigns

31. Give venders your business cards to hand out (lenders, inspec-
    tors, ect.)

32. Go to charity events and meet new people

33. Create and maintain your website profile

34. Work out of state referrals

35. Take care of your current clients (ask for referrals)

36. Prospect in laundromats (usually tentants are there)

37. Work with attorneys to prospect for divorce and estate transactions

38. Send holiday cards

39. Get a wrap or magnetic sign for your car

40. Create videos to promote yourself

41. Host a house warming party for your clients after closing

42. Give your business card to your waitress when you eat out (tip well)

43. Sponsor a little league sports team

44. Walk a neighborhood and put up door hangers

45. Facebook ads

46. Send "Just Sold" postcards to an area to solicit listings

47. Host a tour of homes (multiple open houses)

48. Put your business card in multiple local businesses

49. Maintain your mailing list

50. Engage on Social Media (One of the most powerful prospecting activities)

Social media isn't just for selfies, sunsets, or scrolling. As a Real Estate Agent, it can be your **secret weapon;** a way to stay visible, build trust, and *warm up* cold leads before they even realize they need your help.

Think about it, people do business with those they know, like, and trust. Guess where you can show up consistently, be relatable, and offer value every single day? That's right- Instagram, Facebook, LinkedIn, TikTok, and even YouTube.

However, warming up cold leads doesn't mean spamming your listings or begging people to "DM you for real estate help." It means **strategic connection**. Here's how:

### 1. Be Present, Not Pushy

Show up consistently with content that teaches, inspires, or entertains. Share quick home tips, neighborhood spotlights, success stories, or even behind-the-scenes moments from your real estate journey. When people see you often, they remember you.

### 2. Start Conversations–Not Sales Pitches

Comment on other people's posts. React to stories. Congratulate someone on a life event. These simple interactions warm people up and remind them you exist, without selling a thing.

You're not asking for business. You're building rapport. When they *do* need an agent, you'll be top of mind.

### 3. Build Trust

Treat your social media like a digital open house. You're not just showing properties, you're showing who you are as an agent. Make it easy for people to start trusting you before they ever need you.

**Bottom line:** Cold leads turn warm when you show up, stay real, and offer value before you ask for anything in return. Social media gives you that window. Use it.

# Chapter Sixteen

# "Building Relationships, Not Just a Database"

If there's one thing that can set you apart in a crowded market, it's how you treat people; not just leads, not just closings, people.

Too many new agents focus on building a database before they've built trust, but real estate isn't just about marketing, it's about connections. Every client is a life, every deal is a story, and every opportunity is a chance to serve with integrity.

### Why Relationships Matter More Than Transactions

Statistics show personal referrals significantly outperform online ads in several key areas, with a 37% higher customer retention rate, a 30% higher conversion rate, and a 16% higher lifetime value for customers. Additionally, 92% of consumers trust recommendations from friends and family more than other forms of advertising.

In other words, your relationships are your business.

Clients won't remember the font on your postcard or the filter on your Instagram story. A favorite quote of mine is by, Maya Angelou: "people won't remember what you said or did, but people will never forget how you made them feel."

· Did you listen to them?

· Did you follow up?

· Did you educate without pushing?

· Did you show up with empathy and patience?

Every phone call, every showing, every meeting is a moment to build trust. That trust leads to referrals and referrals lead to longevity.

## Turning Clients Into Lifelong Advocates

Don't let a relationship end at the closing table. Here are practical ways to stay connected:

· Send handwritten thank-you notes after every closing.

· Add past clients to your birthday/holiday calendar.

· Create a quarterly newsletter with tips and market updates.

· Check in six months after the sale just to ask, "How's the house treating you?"

When you care past the paycheck, people notice.

## Referral Systems that Feel Like Real Relationships

You don't need a fancy referral system; you need intentional follow-up. Here are three simple strategies:

· "Client Appreciation Days" - Invite past clients to a free event once a year.

· Pop-by gifts - Small seasonal tokens left at their door (with permission): coffee gift cards, mini planters, etc.

· Social media engagement - Comment on their life updates, not just their home photos. Be human.

**Pro tip:** Every client should know three things by the time you close:

1.  You appreciate them.
2.  You're still here if they need anything.
3.  You'd be honored to serve their friends and family, too.

### Scripts and Starters for Building Trust

Let's be honest, approaching people can feel awkward, but with the right heart and the right words, you can turn strangers into clients without being pushy. Here are some conversation starters:

- "I'm not here to sell you… I'm here to serve you. If you ever need real estate advice or have questions, I'm happy to help."

- "Would it be okay if I kept you in the loop about market updates in your area?"

- "I'm building my business through relationships, not cold calls. I'd love to earn your trust over time."

People respect honesty and humility.

### The Biblical Model of Serving First

Real estate is competitive. But God's Kingdom model is different.

**Philippians 2:3–4** says, *"Do nothing from selfish ambition or conceit, but in humility count others more significant than yourselves. Let each of you look not only to his own interests but also to the interests of others."*

That's the blueprint. Serve first, listen well, show up when it's inconvenient, be generous with your time, be patient when your client is anxious, and always lead with integrity, even if it costs you a deal.

Your reputation isn't just your brand, it's your witness. You're not just building a database, you're building a community. A tribe of people who trust you, respect you, and see Christ in the way you do business. Focus on relationships, and the results will follow.

Serve well, love well, and let your business be a reflection of your faith in action.

# Chapter Seventeen

# "The Power of Multiple Streams of Income"

Real estate is an incredible career path, but it's not always a predictable one. There are seasons of abundance and seasons of drought. One of the wisest things a Realtor can do is diversify their income, not just for financial security, but for long-term freedom.

**Why It Matters**

According to a study from the IRS, the average millionaire has seven streams of income. That's not by accident, it's by design. Multiple income streams protect you from downturns and position you for long-term stability.

In Real Estate deals can fall through, markets can shift, and lets face it, slow months happen. When you have multiple streams of income, you reduce stress and increase sustainability.

## Common Income Streams for Realtors

- **Residential sales** - Your core source of income.

- **Referral income** - Sending business to agents in other cities or specialties.

- **Real Estate Investing** – Buying, flipping, or renting property.

- **Property Management** – Managing homes or units for owners.

- **Teaching/Training** - Sharing knowledge with new agents or running workshops.

- **Home Staging or Design Consulting** - If you have a knack for design, helping sellers prepare homes can become an income-producing service.

- **Speaking, Coaching, or Writing** - Speak with confidence and authority - others will want to learn from you.

### My Journey Into Investment

Within two years of becoming a licensed Realtor, I launched a real estate investment business. Why? I wanted to create wealth, not just income, and real estate gave me an inside edge.

I found my first rental through the MLS. I did much of the labor myself. It stretched me. However, it also taught me that building wealth requires both sweat and vision.

This home now generates a steady income. It's more than just a property; it's part of a legacy I'm building for my family.

## Thinking Beyond The Commission Checks

Here's the truth: Commission checks are great, but they stop when you stop. You need assets and income streams that continue to generate returns, even when you're not actively involved.

Passive income is powerful. It creates margin, gives you options, allows you to be more generous, and it gives you peace of mind during the lean seasons.

Start small, start smart, just start. Don't depend on one source of income alone. Whether it's saving a portion of each commission, investing in a duplex, or simply launching a side business that complements your calling. Pray that if it's in God's will, He will align you with the proper path to take.

## A Biblical Mindset About Wealth

Multiple income streams aren't just about comfort; they're about stewardship.

**Ecclesiastes 11:2** says, *"Invest in seven ventures, yes, in eight; you do not know what disaster may come upon the land."*

God doesn't want you to just survive; He wants you to thrive in a way that allows you to serve others, provide for your family, and fund His Kingdom's work.

Wealth, when submitted to God, becomes a tool, not a trap. You don't have to build seven businesses overnight, but you should be thinking long-term. Commission checks are a blessing, they're not the only way God can provide for us. Let your income reflect your innovation, let your strategy reflect your stewardship, and let your success reflect the Source. **Where God calls, He provides, but He also expects you to prepare.**

# Chapter Eighteen

# "Built on Faith – Daily Devotionals"

In the Real Estate World, your days can feel long, unpredictable, and emotionally heavy. The pressure to perform, produce, and provide can quietly wear you down, unless you're anchored in something deeper.

That "something deeper" is Christ Jesus. If your career is going to stand the test of time, it must be built on a solid foundation of faith.

Here are five daily devotionals specifically tailored for Real Estate Professionals. Let these words remind you of who you are and who you belong to.

**Day 1: You're Called**

**Scripture:** *"Whatever you do, work at it with all your heart, as working for the Lord, not for men." – Colossians 3:23*

You may have earned your real estate license, but your calling came from God. You weren't placed in this business by accident. Whether your path was dramatic or quiet, God has equipped you for such a time as this. Let that truth reshape how you see your clients, your schedule, and your success. You're not working for approval or applause, you're working in obedience to the One who sent you.

**Prayer:** *Lord, remind me today that I was called to this business. Help me work with excellence, not for people's approval, but for Your glory. Amen.*

### Day 2: Trust in the Unknown

**Scripture:** *"Trust in the Lord with all your heart and lean not on your own understanding." – Proverbs 3:5*

In real estate, there's so much you can't control… buyers back out, deals fall apart, and leads go quiet. Just the same, faith isn't about control; it's about trust. Today, let go of the pressure to predict or manage every outcome. God knows what you need before you even ask. Your job is obedience. His job is provision.

**Prayer:** *Jesus, help me release what I can't control. I trust You with the outcomes. Strengthen my faith in the waiting. Amen.*

### Day 3: God Goes Before You

**Scripture:** *"The Lord himself goes before you and will be with you; he will never leave you nor forsake you." – Deuteronomy 31:8*

Before you walk into that listing appointment… God is already there. Before you make that phone call… He's preparing the heart on the other end. You are never walking alone. Take a moment today to acknowledge His presence in your business. Invite Him into your meetings, your client conversations, and even your doubts. He's not just beside you, He's ahead of you.

**Prayer:** *Father, go before me today. Prepare the path, soften hearts, and guide my every step. I trust that You're already working. Amen.*

**Day 4:Integrity Over Income**

**Scripture:** *"Better is a little with righteousness than great revenues with injustice." – Proverbs 16:8*

Real Estate can tempt you to cut corners, exaggerate value, or bend truth for the sake of a deal. But your character is more valuable than any commission check. Choose integrity, especially when no one is watching. Honor God with your ethics. He will bless what's done in righteousness.

**Prayer:** *God, help me to be honest, upright, and dependable. Let me never sacrifice my witness for a win. Make my business a reflection of Your truth. Amen.*

**Day 5: Provision in Every Season**

**Scripture:** *"Look at the birds of the air; they do not sow or reap or store away in barns, and yet your heavenly Father feeds them." – Matthew 6:26*

Slow seasons are real. They test your faith and question your calling. Remember God sees you, He knows your needs, and He's never stopped providing. Rest in His faithfulness. Don't confuse silence with absence. Even now, God is working behind the scenes to bring about divine appointments and unexpected opportunities.

**Prayer:** *Jehovah Jireh, my Provider, thank You for always taking care of me. I trust You in the abundance and in the quiet. I know You have good plans. Amen.*

These devotionals are more than encouragement; they're fuel. Keep them close, speak them aloud, and let them shape the spiritual foundation of your real estate career. When your business is built on faith, no market shift can shake it.

# Chapter Nineteen

# "Faith in the Storm: Thriving in a Difficult Market"

It's easy to feel confident when the market is strong. Closings are steady, leads are flowing, and income seems almost predictable. In those seasons, it's tempting to assume the momentum will never slow, and sometimes we forget the wisdom of Joseph in Egypt, who stored grain in the plentiful years to survive the lean ones.

When the market is good, saving feels optional. When the market shifts, that lack of preparation can shake even the most confident agent. I learned this lesson firsthand. When my business was thriving, I was grateful, but I didn't save as much as I should have. When the market slowed I felt it, hard. Showings dried up, buyers grew cautious, listings lingered, and the commission checks I had grown accustomed to vanished for a time.

It wasn't just financially stressful, it was emotionally exhausting. This turned out to be sacred ground. In that storm, God wasn't silent. He was strengthening me.

Here are a few key points to help you in a challenging market.

### Keep Showing Up

When business slows, the temptation is to retreat. But this is when consistency matters most.

- Keep prospecting.
- Keep following up.
- Keep learning.
- Keep praying.

Success in a slow market doesn't usually look like big wins. It looks like quiet faithfulness, small seeds, daily discipline, and a heart that refuses to quit.

### Simplify, Then Strengthen

Use market slowdowns to:

- Audit your business expenses.
- Streamline your systems.
- Refresh your branding and marketing plan.
- Deepen relationships with your current database.

You don't need more noise, you need more focus. God slows things down to remove distractions to help you regain focus on Him.

### Speak Life Over Your Business

Don't talk about how bad the market is, speak life over your work. Speak scripture, speak vision.

**Proverbs 18:21** says, *"The tongue has the power of life and death."*

Your words matter. Declare God's promises over your career, Prophesy growth and believe in breakthrough. Every morning during that difficult season, I'd say out loud:

*"God, You are my source. Not the market. Not the economy. You. You go before me. You bring the increase. I trust You."*

Slowly, but surely, He did.

### Lean Into Community

This is not the time to isolate. Stay plugged in with other faith-filled agents, your broker, or a mentor. Be honest about your struggles, share your wins, and pray for one another. The enemy loves to isolate you when you're vulnerable. But God designed us for community.

**Ecclesiastes 4:9–10** says, *"Two are better than one… if either of them falls, one can help the other up."*

### Remember Your Why

When deals dry up, it's easy to question your calling, but complex markets don't mean God changed His mind. Go back to the journal entry, the prayer, or the moment when God called you to this. He's still with you, still has a plan, and you're still right where you need to be. Difficult markets don't last forever, but faithful agents do. Your current struggle might be preparing you for a greater season of impact. Don't lose heart, dig deeper, stay grounded, and remember: **The storm isn't where your story ends. It's where your faith grows stronger.**

# Chapter Twenty

# "Standing Firm When It's Hard"

There's a side of business that no one talks about in training, the unseen battle. The war between doing what's right and doing what's easy. Between honoring God and feeding your flesh. It's real, it's constant, and if you're not rooted in your faith, it can shake you.

I remember one transaction early in my career that brought this to life in a way I'll never forget. I was working with another experienced, confident, and persuasive agent. We were co-representing clients in a deal that was already showing signs of stress. Paperwork delays, miscommunications, and tension on both sides.

Then came the moment. There was a document that required handling in a particular way, both legally and ethically. The other agent didn't want to do it that way. She said, "It's no big deal. We can simply sign, scan, and backdate it. It'll make everything easier." Everything in me tightened.

On paper, it would've made my life easier. Fewer phone calls, less back-and-forth, the deal would close faster.

My client probably wouldn't have known the difference, but I would've known, and more importantly God would've known.

I took a deep breath and said, "I can't do that." She didn't like that at all. The rest of the deal was tense with cold emails and sharp tones. It felt like she was trying to punish me for not playing along. I'll be honest, there were moments I wanted to cave. I wanted to snap back. I wanted to defend myself and justify my actions, to show that I was doing the right thing. Every time I got ready to respond in my flesh, the Holy Spirit would whisper: *"You represent Me first."*

So I stayed quiet, when I could've fired back. I stayed kind when I was met with coldness and I kept my hands clean, even when it made things more complicated. When that transaction finally closed, I was exhausted, but I was also at peace. I knew that I didn't only complete a deal, I had passed a test.

## Spiritual Growth Through Resistance

That experience reminded me: spiritual warfare isn't always dramatic, sometimes it's subtle. It shows up in the small compromises. The quiet corners we think no one sees, but God does. When you choose Him, even when it's costly, He honors that.

Sometimes integrity will make you stand out, other times it will cost you influence, relationships, or even deals. Nothing is worth more than your witness.

**Ephesians 6:13** *says, "Put on the full armor of God, so that when the day of evil comes, you may be able to stand your ground."*

I didn't win anything that day in the eyes of man but in the Kingdom? I stood my ground. That's a victory I'll never regret.

In Real Estate and in life you'll face moments where the pressure to conform is loud, especially these days. Don't bend, stand firm, and lead with honor. Do the right thing, even if you stand alone.

At the end of the day, we're not just Realtors, we're representatives of Christ, and the deal isn't worth your witness.

Walking with integrity and honoring God in every transaction doesn't stay confined to your work life. It seeps into everything: your relationships, your habits, your decisions. What starts in business will begin to shape your character. You'll find yourself:

·   Wanting to speak more truthfully.
·   Thinking twice before reacting.
·   Choosing peace over retaliation.
·   Respecting others even when you feel they don't deserve it.

It's not about perfection, it's about pursuit. Pursuing righteousness not just at the closing table, but at the dinner table, at the gas station, with your kids, with strangers.

**Psalm 15:2–5 says:** *"The one whose walk is blameless, who does what is righteous, who speaks the truth from their heart; whose tongue utters no slander, who does no wrong to a neighbor, and casts no slur on others; who despises a vile person but honors those who fear the Lord; who keeps an oath even when it hurts, and does not change their mind; who lends money to the poor without interest; who does not accept a bribe against the innocent. Whoever does these things will never be shaken."*

That is the life we're called to, not just in business, but in every step we take. Walk upright, do what is right, even when no one's looking, and trust that when your foundation is integrity, you will not be shaken.

# Chapter Twenty-One

# "From Broken to Built"

When I was 19, I thought I had the whole world in my hands. I was young, driven, full of energy, and convinced I was on a path that would take me anywhere I wanted to go. That same year, I got married for the first time. We were just kids, hopeful and well-intentioned, but unprepared for the road ahead.

It wasn't long after I started my career in the delivery business that things began to change. We grew apart, life pulled us in different directions, and eventually, our marriage came to an end. It was a painful chapter, one I wouldn't want to relive but even in that season of brokenness God was already working.

There are two things from that marriage that I will be forever grateful for. First, we had some incredible kids together. They've been a light in my life, and I wouldn't trade them for anything. Second, maybe even more unexpected, I was introduced to the One who would change my life forever.. In the midst of my youth, my pride and my mess, she pointed me toward salvation in Jesus. That alone changed the entire trajectory of my life.

Looking back now, I see it more clearly than ever: God wastes nothing. He can use even our broken beginnings to build something beautiful.

There was a season after that divorce when I hit what I now know was rock bottom. At the time, I didn't have the words to describe it; I just knew I was angry not just with the world, but with God. Somewhere deep inside, I held Him responsible for the pain I was in. I had given my life to Him so why had everything still fallen apart? That bitterness took root, I didn't see it happening at first, but the enemy crept in little by little. The tiny crack in my faith became a wide open door.

I started drinking more and searching for anything that could numb the ache inside me. I was trying to fill a void that only God could fill, but I was running from the very One who could heal me. The devil doesn't always kick the door in; sometimes he waits for us to open it just a little and that is exactly what I did.

That season of my life was dark. I was still showing up to work, still going through the motions, but inside I was unraveling. The passion I once had for life, the hope I had found in Christ, it all felt distant. Even then... God never left me. I left Him. I stopped going to church, stopped praying, and stopped opening my Bible. Anything that had once connected me to God, I walked away from it.

In my heart, I believed He had taken everything from me. I couldn't make sense of the pain, and instead of trusting Him with it, I turned the pain into blame. I can still hear myself, lying in bed alone one night, staring at the ceiling and whispering those words with bitterness in my chest: *"The Lord giveth and the Lord taketh away."*

It was a verse I had once found comfort in but that night, it felt like a cruel truth. I had accepted the One who gave me life... and in return, I felt like He took everything I had worked so hard to build. I couldn't understand it then, and honestly I didn't want to.

I didn't want comfort or correction; I just wanted to be angry. Anger was easier than vulnerability and it was easier than surrender.

Even in the season of rejection… God remained. He never pulled away. He never gave up on me. He just waited. Patiently, silently, and lovingly, He waited for the moment when I'd finally stop trying to build my life on my own broken foundation… and come back to the One who could truly rebuild it.

I recall being at one of the lowest points in my life and thinking, *'This is it.' Where do I go from here?* Everything felt lost, directionless, like I had fallen into a pit so deep that no light could reach me. I wasn't just questioning my future, I was questioning if there was any future left at all. What I didn't realize is even in that silence, even in the heavy ache of rock bottom, God was already working. Quietly, steadily, lovingly, He was moving in the background, setting things in motion to pull me out of the darkness.

Sometimes He doesn't come to our rescue with flashing lights or booming voices. Sometimes He plants small seeds. Delicate little signs of His presence. A conversation, a phone call, a memory, a moment of unexpected peace in the middle of the chaos. It's those seeds, small as they may seem, that begin to sprout in the soul and pull us out of the abyss. One moment at a time, one breath at a time, and one whisper of grace at a time.

That's what He did for me. He didn't do it through a lightning bolt or some dramatic intervention. He did it in a completely unexpected way… through my kids. Even in all the mess I had created, through the alcohol, the women, the late nights, the empty pursuits… there was one constant that never stopped tugging at my heart: my children. They were always there. A mirror to the man I wanted to be, a reminder of the man I was created to be.

While I was running *from* God, they were running *toward* Him. They were deeply involved in their church, fully committed to their walk with Christ. Even though I was far from where I needed to be, their example quietly echoed in my spirit.

I'll never forget one particular day. I had just gotten off a long shift at work. Tired, numb, just scrolling through Facebook, looking for something to distract me. Then I saw it. It wasn't flashy or loud; it was just a simple picture. My kids, sitting in a circle at church, heads bowed in prayer. That was it, but that picture hit me like a tidal wave. The thought hit me so clearly, it was almost audible: *"I wonder if they're praying for me?"*

That tiny seed, planted in a casual scroll on social media, was the beginning of something holy. That was the moment something shifted in me. A picture of my children doing something so simple brought me face-to-face with the grace of God. That image pulled me out of the fog. It reminded me that there was still hope, still purpose, still a calling over my life. Slowly, it led me back to the Father.

Today my faith and conviction in Christ is stronger than it's ever been, and it all started with a picture… and the unshakable faith of my children. That moment, seeing my kids praying, realizing how far I had drifted and how gently God was pulling me back, taught me something I'll never forget: <u>Faith is everything.</u>

Not just faith for miracles or for the mountains to move, but faith that God is still present in the quiet. Faith that He's still working when nothing makes sense. Faith that He hasn't given up on you, even when you've given up on yourself. Faith isn't just a belief. It's a posture, a surrender, a lifeline.

It was faith that helped me take the first step back toward Jesus, even when I wasn't sure if I'd be welcomed.

It was faith that helped me believe He could still use me, after everything I'd done and all the ways I had failed Him. It was faith that showed me He didn't just want to fix me… He wanted to rebuild me. Piece by piece, from the ground up.

The truth is, I've come to realize that faith isn't built in the good times; it's forged in the fire. It's in the struggle, the silence, in the waiting where real faith is shaped. *"Now faith is the substance of things hoped for, the evidence of things not seen."* **Hebrews 11:1**

I couldn't always see what God was doing but He was still doing it, and if He did it for me… He can do it for you too. So how does all of this… every broken moment, every dark night, every quiet prayer, tie back to Real Estate? It's simple: **Faith changes everything.**

Faith isn't just what brought me through the pain, it's what equipped me to stand confidently in my purpose. It made me a better man, a better father… and yes, a better Realtor. When you've walked through fire and come out the other side, you carry a compassion that can't be taught.

You understand struggle, so you sit longer with a nervous first-time buyer. You know what it means to wait, so you walk with patience through slow escrows and tough negotiations. You've seen what it looks like to rebuild from nothing, so you cheer louder when your client finds their dream home or their second chance.

Faith doesn't just make you spiritually stronger; it sharpens your character. It makes you dependable. It makes you honest. It makes you bold in the face of fear. More than anything, faith anchors you when the market shifts, when deals fall through, when life throws you another curveball. Your identity isn't in your closings… It's in Christ.

This business will stretch you, it will test you, but if it's built on faith… real, tested, God-shaped faith, you won't just survive. You will thrive. You will build something eternal, one closing at a time.

Let me leave you with this: You don't have to be perfect to be used, you just have to be willing. God can take your brokenness and build a testimony that speaks louder than any marketing strategy. He can take your past and turn it into purpose. He can take your Real Estate License… and turn it into a ministry.

If He did it for me… He can do it for you.

So walk by faith, build with integrity, love your clients well, and never forget… *"Unless the Lord builds the house, the builders labor in vain."* **- Psalm 127:1**

Let your career be built, not just on leads or systems, but on faith. Because when it is, nothing can shake it. Not even you.

# Chapter Twenty-Two

# Final Thought To You, the Reader... The One Who's Still Building

I want to tell you something straight from my heart: You were made for more.

You're not just here to close deals or climb a leaderboard. You're here to build something eternal, to walk into rooms with authority because the Spirit of God walks in with you. To love people when they're hard to love, and to stand firm when no one else will. You're here to show the world what it looks like to do business God's way, with honesty, humility, and fierce faith.

You may feel like you're still in the middle of your mess. You may feel like you're behind, like you missed your chance. Let me tell you this: **You haven't missed a thing.** <u>**The God who called you still has plans for you.**</u>

Here's what I challenge you to do:

· Wake up every day and choose integrity, even when it costs you.

· Pray over your clients, even when they never know.

· Keep learning, keep growing, and keep showing up when it's hard.

· Trust God not just for the next deal, but for the entire journey.

And never forget this: **<u>Your calling is bigger than your commission.</u>**

You are more than a Realtor. You are a Kingdom builder.

So go out there and build with boldness, build with love, and above all… **<u>build with faith.</u>**

# Acknowledgements

First and foremost, I give thanks to God, for His countless blessings, for His unwavering presence in my life, and for carrying me through even the moments when I couldn't feel Him near.

To my wife Laci, the net that caught me when I was falling. Your love, strength, and devotion has sustained me more than words can express. I am forever grateful for the grace and love you bring into my life.

To my children Braden, Mikyla, and Logan who reminded me often without knowing, that God was always there, working in quiet powerful ways. Through you, I found strength and clarity during times of doubt.

To my adopted children - Faith, Abbie, and Josh, thank you for welcoming me into your lives as a father figure. I know I could never take the place of your own, but please know that I love you as if you were my own. I can't imagine my life without each of you in it.

To my grandchildren Isaiah, Ezra, Adeline, Karsyn, Kambry, Selah, Willow, and Walker whose unconditional love shines brightly like the light of Christ, thank you for filling my days with joy, wonder, and hope. May God bless your lives always! Pops loves you!

# About the author

Blake Osman is an Arkansas Realtor by day and a storyteller at heart. When he's not helping people find their perfect home, he's crafting imaginative and unforgettable characters. His debut children's book, Otis the Squirrel and the City Adventure, marks the beginning of a long-awaited journey into the world of publishing. With a treasure trove of stories written over the years, Blake has plans to bring many more to life, spanning genres from fantasy and young adult to thrillers and romance. Under a secret pen name, he explores the full spectrum of fiction, always chasing the next great tale.

Blake was recognized as the Realtor of the Year at the 2025 Community Choice Awards Fort Smith and honored to receive the Community Votes Fort Smith Platinum Winner award for Best in Real Estate in 2024. His success can be attributed to his honesty, authenticity, and genuine passion for helping people, qualities rooted in his faith, that have enabled him to build lasting relationships and trust with every client.

# Also by

## Blake Osman

**AVAILABLE NOW**

**Children's Book:** *"Otis The Squirrel And The City Adventure"*

**COMING SPRING 2026**

**Childrens Book:** *"The Courage Hat"*

**COMING FALL 2026**

**Contemporary Romance:** *"In The Time We Have"*

Join Blake's newsletter at his author websites:

BlakeOsmanBooks.com

BlakeOsman.com

Follow me on Social Media! Links on Author Websites!

Please take the time to leave a honest review of this book.
You can do so by searching it on Amazon.com, go towards the
bottom of the page and you should see "write a review."
Thank you for your support!